EMMANUEL JOSEPH

Artificial Dreams, Eternal Callings
Balancing Career, Love, and Faith in the
Digital Age

Copyright © 2025 by Emmanuel Joseph

All rights reserved. No part of this publication may be reproduced, stored or transmitted in any form or by any means, electronic, mechanical, photocopying, recording, scanning, or otherwise without written permission from the publisher. It is illegal to copy this book, post it to a website, or distribute it by any other means without permission.

First edition

This book was professionally typeset on Reedsy.
Find out more at reedsy.com

Contents

1	Chapter 1: Genesis of the Digital Dream	1
2	Chapter 2: The Intersection of Love and Career	3
3	Chapter 3: Faith in the Digital Era	5
4	Chapter 4: Navigating Career Peaks and Valleys	7
5	Chapter 5: The Evolution of Love	9
6	Chapter 6: Faith's Guiding Light	10
7	Chapter 7: Embracing Change and Growth	11
8	Chapter 8: Building a Legacy	12
9	Chapter 9: Love in the Digital Age	13
10	Chapter 10: The Power of Faith	14
11	Chapter 11: Embracing the Future	15
12	Chapter 12: A Legacy of Balance	16
13	Chapter 13: Harmonizing Work and Passion	18
14	Chapter 14: The Digital Disconnect	20
15	Chapter 15: Mentorship and Legacy	21
16	Chapter 16: Embracing Parenthood	22
17	Chapter 17: The Future of the Digital Age	23

1

Chapter 1: Genesis of the Digital Dream

In a world where technology bridges continents and timezones, Olanna felt both blessed and cursed. Her career in the bustling tech hub of Lagos placed her at the frontier of innovation. Every new project felt like stepping into uncharted territory, where she could create, invent, and inspire. Yet, as the days turned into nights, she wondered if the incessant hum of her laptop was drowning out the quieter yearnings of her heart.

Olanna's journey into the tech world was almost predestined. Growing up, her home was filled with the latest gadgets, courtesy of her tech-savvy father. While her peers played outside, Olanna was engrossed in coding, learning the language of the future. However, the more she immersed herself in this artificial realm, the more she felt the disconnect from the tactile, human experiences that once brought her joy.

Her friends, though proud of her achievements, often teased her about being married to her job. Late-night calls and early morning meetings became the norm. Olanna's ambitions were vast, but so were her fears of losing herself to the very world she was helping to shape. The digital dream was a double-edged sword, offering both liberation and confinement.

In those quiet moments, Olanna turned to her faith for solace. She attended church services, finding comfort in the age-old rituals and hymns. Here, amidst the congregation, she felt a sense of belonging that the virtual world could never offer. It was in these moments of reflection that she began to question her path, seeking a balance between her career aspirations, love, and spiritual fulfillment.

2

Chapter 2: The Intersection of Love and Career

Love, they say, finds you when you least expect it. For Olanna, it came in the form of Kelechi, a fellow tech enthusiast with a heart as vast as his intellect. Their paths crossed during a tech conference, and what began as a shared passion for innovation soon blossomed into a deeper connection. Yet, the digital age posed its own set of challenges to their budding romance.

Both driven by their careers, Olanna and Kelechi often found themselves on opposite ends of the globe, attending different conferences, launching new products, and pushing the boundaries of what was possible. The virtual meetings and video calls, while convenient, could never replace the warmth of a shared moment in person. The digital tools that connected them also highlighted the distances between them.

Olanna cherished the moments they could steal away from their hectic schedules. Weekend getaways and late-night conversations became their sanctuaries. However, the pressures of their careers loomed large, casting shadows over their shared dreams. Olanna often wondered if their love could withstand the relentless pace of the tech world.

Amidst these challenges, their love grew stronger. They learned to navigate the complexities of their careers while nurturing their bond. Kelechi's unwavering support and understanding became Olanna's anchor, grounding her amidst the chaos. Together, they began to envision a future where their dreams of career success and a fulfilling relationship could coexist.

3

Chapter 3: Faith in the Digital Era

Olanna's faith had always been a guiding light, offering her clarity and strength in times of uncertainty. However, in the fast-paced digital age, maintaining that connection became increasingly challenging. The constant barrage of information, the demands of her career, and the pursuit of love often left little room for introspection and spiritual growth.

She found solace in her church community, where she could disconnect from the digital noise and reconnect with her inner self. The rituals, the prayers, and the sense of belonging offered her a sanctuary from the relentless pace of her life. Yet, Olanna knew that faith was not just about attending services; it was about integrating those values into her daily existence.

Her relationship with Kelechi also became a spiritual journey. They often discussed their beliefs, finding common ground and supporting each other's spiritual growth. Their faith became a pillar of their relationship, offering them strength and resilience in the face of challenges. Together, they attended church services, participated in community events, and found ways to give back to society.

Balancing faith in the digital age required conscious effort. Olanna began to set aside time for daily reflections, prayer, and meditation. She realized that while technology offered countless advantages, it was crucial to create boundaries to preserve her spiritual well-being. Faith, love, and career were not mutually exclusive; they could coexist harmoniously if nurtured with care and intention.

4

Chapter 4: Navigating Career Peaks and Valleys

Olanna's career trajectory was a rollercoaster ride, filled with exhilarating highs and daunting lows. Each new project, each innovation, brought with it a sense of accomplishment and pride. Yet, the pressures and challenges were equally immense. There were moments of doubt, setbacks, and failures that tested her resolve and determination.

In the fast-paced tech world, success was often measured by the latest breakthrough or the next big thing. Olanna found herself constantly striving for excellence, sometimes at the cost of her well-being. The late nights, the stress, and the relentless pursuit of perfection took a toll on her mental and physical health. It was during these challenging times that she leaned on her support system for strength.

Kelechi, with his unwavering belief in her abilities, became her rock. His words of encouragement and his presence provided the reassurance she needed to keep pushing forward. Olanna also turned to her faith, finding solace in prayer and reflection. The valleys in her career journey became opportunities for growth and self-discovery.

Navigating the peaks and valleys required a delicate balance. Olanna learned to celebrate her successes while remaining grounded and humble. She also embraced the challenges, viewing them as opportunities to learn and evolve. Through it all, she realized that her career was just one aspect of her identity. Her relationships, faith, and personal well-being were equally important and deserving of attention.

5

Chapter 5: The Evolution of Love

As the years passed, Olanna and Kelechi's love evolved, deepening and maturing with each new experience. They learned to navigate the complexities of their individual careers while nurturing their relationship. Love, they discovered, was not just about grand gestures but about the small, everyday moments that wove their lives together.

They faced challenges head-on, supporting each other through career transitions, relocations, and personal growth. The digital tools that once seemed to create distance between them now became bridges, allowing them to stay connected despite physical separations. Video calls, text messages, and virtual dates became integral parts of their relationship.

Olanna and Kelechi also found joy in shared experiences. They traveled together, exploring new cultures and creating lasting memories. Their adventures, both big and small, strengthened their bond and brought them closer. They learned to find balance, ensuring that their careers did not overshadow their relationship.

The evolution of their love was a testament to their commitment and resilience. They understood that love required effort, compromise, and unwavering support. Together, they built a life where their dreams of career success, love, and faith coexisted harmoniously. Their journey was not without its challenges, but it was marked by a deep sense of fulfillment and joy.

6

Chapter 6: Faith's Guiding Light

Faith continued to play a central role in Olanna's life, guiding her decisions and offering her strength in times of uncertainty. In the digital age, where distractions were abundant, maintaining a strong spiritual connection required conscious effort. Olanna made it a priority to nurture her faith, integrating it into her daily routine.

She found ways to blend her faith with her career, seeking opportunities to give back to her community and make a positive impact. Olanna's faith became a source of inspiration, driving her to use her skills and knowledge for the greater good. She volunteered at local organizations, mentored young professionals, and advocated for ethical practices in the tech industry.

Her relationship with Kelechi also benefited from their shared faith. They attended church services together, participated in community events, and supported each other's spiritual growth. Their faith became a pillar of their relationship, offering them strength and resilience in the face of challenges.

Faith, Olanna realized, was not just about rituals and traditions; it was about living her values every day. It was about being kind, compassionate, and making a positive impact on the world. Her faith guided her actions, helping her navigate the complexities of the digital age with grace and integrity.

7

Chapter 7: Embracing Change and Growth

Change was a constant in Olanna's life, both in her career and personal journey. The tech world was ever-evolving, demanding adaptability and resilience. Olanna embraced change, viewing it as an opportunity for growth and self-discovery. She learned to navigate new technologies, take on different roles, and continuously expand her skillset.

Her relationship with Kelechi also evolved, growing stronger with each new experience. They supported each other's personal and professional growth, understanding that change was an inevitable part of life. Together, they faced new challenges, celebrated milestones, and adapted to the shifting dynamics of their relationship.

Olanna's faith provided her with a sense of stability amidst the constant changes. It reminded her of the values that anchored her, offering her a guiding light in times of uncertainty. Faith, love, and career were not static; they were dynamic, evolving with each new chapter of her life.

Embracing change required a mindset of openness and curiosity. Olanna learned to let go of fear and embrace the unknown. She viewed each change as an opportunity to learn, grow, and become a better version of herself. Through it all, she remained grounded in her values, navigating the complexities of the digital age with grace and resilience.

8

Chapter 8: Building a Legacy

As Olanna's career continued to flourish, she began to think about the legacy she wanted to leave behind. She realized that success was not just about personal achievements but about making a meaningful impact on the world. Olanna's experiences had taught her the importance of balance, and she was determined to share those lessons with others.

She began to mentor young professionals, offering guidance and support as they navigated their own career journeys. Olanna shared her insights on balancing career, love, and faith, emphasizing the importance of staying true to one's values. Her mentees admired her wisdom and resilience, drawing inspiration from her journey.

Olanna also became an advocate for diversity and inclusion in the tech industry. She recognized the need for representation and equal opportunities for all. Through her efforts, she worked to create a more inclusive environment where everyone could thrive. Olanna's legacy was not just about her achievements but about the positive change she inspired in others.

Her relationship with Kelechi remained a cornerstone of her life. Together, they continued to support each other's dreams while building a future rooted in love and faith. Olanna's journey was a testament to the power of balance and the importance of staying true to oneself. Her legacy was a reflection of her values, her resilience, and her unwavering commitment to making a difference.

9

Chapter 9: Love in the Digital Age

The digital age brought both opportunities and challenges to Olanna and Kelechi's relationship. While technology allowed them to stay connected, it also presented new dynamics that required careful navigation. They learned to find a balance between their virtual interactions and real-life moments, ensuring that their relationship remained strong and meaningful.

Olanna and Kelechi embraced the digital tools at their disposal, using them to bridge the gaps created by their busy schedules. They scheduled virtual dates, sent each other thoughtful messages, and stayed connected through video calls. These efforts allowed them to maintain their bond despite the physical distances that often separated them.

However, they also recognized the importance of disconnecting from the digital world to nurture their relationship. They made it a point to spend quality time together, enjoying activities that brought them joy and strengthened their connection. Whether it was a weekend getaway or a simple walk in the park, these moments became the foundation of their love.

Their journey in the digital age was a testament to their commitment and adaptability. Olanna and Kelechi learned to navigate the complexities of their relationship while staying true to their values. Their love thrived in the digital age, a harmonious blend of virtual and real-life interactions that brought them closer together.

10

Chapter 10: The Power of Faith

Faith remained a guiding force in Olanna's life, offering her strength and clarity in times of uncertainty. In the digital age, maintaining a strong spiritual connection required conscious effort. Olanna made it a priority to nurture her faith, integrating it into her daily routine and finding ways to live her values.

Her faith guided her decisions, helping her navigate the complexities of her career and personal life. Olanna found solace in prayer and reflection, using these moments to find clarity and direction. She also sought out opportunities to give back to her community, using her skills and resources to make a positive impact.

Olanna's relationship with Kelechi was also strengthened by their shared faith. They supported each other's spiritual growth, attending church services together and participating in community events. Their faith became a pillar of their relationship, offering them strength and resilience in the face of challenges.

Faith, Olanna realized, was not just about rituals and traditions; it was about living her values every day. It was about being kind, compassionate, and making a positive impact on the world. Her faith guided her actions, helping her navigate the complexities of the digital age with grace and integrity.

11

Chapter 11: Embracing the Future

As Olanna and Kelechi looked towards the future, they remained committed to their dreams and values. The digital age presented new opportunities and challenges, but they were prepared to face them together. They continued to support each other's careers while nurturing their relationship and faith.

Olanna's career continued to evolve, bringing new opportunities for growth and innovation. She remained dedicated to making a positive impact in the tech industry, advocating for diversity and inclusion. Her legacy of balance, resilience, and compassion continued to inspire those around her.

Kelechi's journey was equally fulfilling, as he pursued his own dreams while supporting Olanna. Together, they built a life rooted in love, faith, and mutual respect. Their journey was a testament to the power of balance and the importance of staying true to oneself.

As they embraced the future, Olanna and Kelechi remained committed to their values. They understood that the digital age required adaptability and resilience, and they were prepared to navigate its complexities with grace and integrity. Their journey was a reflection of their commitment to each other, their faith, and their dreams.

12

Chapter 12: A Legacy of Balance

Olanna and Kelechi's journey was a testament to the power of balance in the digital age. They had navigated the complexities of their careers while nurturing their relationship and faith. Their story was one of resilience, adaptability, and unwavering commitment to their values.

As they looked back on their journey, Olanna and Kelechi realized that their greatest achievement was not their individual successes but the life they had built together. They had created a legacy of balance, where career, love, and faith coexisted harmoniously. Their journey had inspired others to seek their own balance, to stay true to their values, and to embrace the opportunities of the digital age.

Olanna's legacy extended beyond her career. She had made a meaningful impact on the world, inspiring others to pursue their dreams while staying grounded in their values. Her journey was a testament to the power of resilience, compassion, and balance.

Kelechi's support and unwavering belief in Olanna had been a cornerstone of their journey. Together, they had built a life that reflected their dreams and values. Their legacy was a reflection of their love, their faith, and their commitment to making a positive impact on the world.

In the end, Olanna and Kelechi's story was a reminder that balance is the key to a fulfilling life. The digital age may bring new challenges, but with

CHAPTER 12: A LEGACY OF BALANCE

faith, love, and resilience, it is possible to navigate its complexities and create a legacy of harmony and purpose. Their journey was a testament to the power of balance in the digital age, inspiring others to seek their own path and embrace the opportunities that lie ahead.

add more 5 chapter

13

Chapter 13: Harmonizing Work and Passion

Olanna's work in the tech industry was more than just a job; it was her passion. However, she understood the importance of finding a balance between work and personal passions. She sought ways to integrate her hobbies and interests into her busy schedule, ensuring that her life was fulfilling on multiple levels.

One of Olanna's passions was music. She had always loved playing the piano and found solace in creating melodies. Despite her demanding career, she made time for her musical pursuits, joining a local band and performing at community events. Music became a form of therapy, allowing her to express herself and find joy outside of her professional responsibilities.

Her relationship with Kelechi also thrived as they discovered new shared interests. They took up cooking together, experimenting with different cuisines and bonding over their culinary creations. These moments of shared passion strengthened their connection and provided a much-needed respite from their busy lives.

Finding harmony between work and personal passions required conscious effort. Olanna learned to prioritize her well-being, ensuring that her passions were an integral part of her life. This balance allowed her to bring her best self to both her career and her relationship, creating a life that was rich and

CHAPTER 13: HARMONIZING WORK AND PASSION

fulfilling.

14

Chapter 14: The Digital Disconnect

In the age of constant connectivity, Olanna realized the importance of disconnecting from the digital world to reconnect with herself and those around her. The demands of her career often required her to be constantly online, but she knew that true balance required moments of unplugged serenity.

Olanna began to set boundaries, designating specific times to disconnect from her devices. She embraced the simplicity of offline activities, such as hiking, reading, and spending quality time with loved ones. These moments of digital detox allowed her to recharge and gain a fresh perspective on her life.

Kelechi also supported Olanna's efforts to disconnect. They planned regular getaways to nature, where they could escape the digital noise and immerse themselves in the beauty of the natural world. These retreats became cherished memories, offering them a chance to deepen their connection and find peace.

The digital disconnect was not just about turning off devices; it was about being present in the moment and appreciating the world around her. Olanna learned that true balance required intentional efforts to disconnect, allowing her to find clarity, peace, and a deeper connection to her faith and loved ones.

15

Chapter 15: Mentorship and Legacy

As Olanna's career progressed, she felt a deep sense of responsibility to mentor the next generation of tech professionals. She understood the challenges and pressures they faced and wanted to share her experiences and insights to help them navigate their own journeys.

Olanna became a mentor to young professionals, offering guidance, support, and encouragement. She shared her story of balancing career, love, and faith, emphasizing the importance of staying true to one's values. Her mentees admired her resilience and wisdom, drawing inspiration from her journey.

In addition to mentorship, Olanna also advocated for creating a more inclusive and diverse tech industry. She worked tirelessly to promote equal opportunities and representation for all, believing that diversity was essential for innovation and progress. Her efforts made a meaningful impact, inspiring positive change within the industry.

Olanna's legacy extended beyond her professional achievements. She was remembered for her compassion, integrity, and dedication to making a difference. Her journey was a testament to the power of balance and the importance of staying true to one's values. Through her mentorship and advocacy, Olanna left a lasting legacy that inspired others to pursue their dreams and make a positive impact on the world.

16

Chapter 16: Embracing Parenthood

As Olanna and Kelechi's relationship deepened, they began to discuss the possibility of starting a family. The prospect of parenthood brought both excitement and uncertainty, as they considered how to balance their careers, love, and faith with the responsibilities of raising children.

They approached the decision with thoughtful consideration, discussing their values, dreams, and priorities. Olanna and Kelechi wanted to create a nurturing and loving environment for their future children, where they could grow and thrive. They sought to instill the importance of balance, resilience, and faith in their family.

Parenthood brought new challenges and joys into their lives. Olanna and Kelechi learned to navigate the complexities of raising children while maintaining their careers and nurturing their relationship. They found support in their faith, drawing strength from their shared values and community.

Embracing parenthood required adaptability and a commitment to finding balance. Olanna and Kelechi worked together as a team, supporting each other through the highs and lows of parenting. Their journey was a testament to their love, resilience, and unwavering commitment to creating a life rooted in faith and balance.

17

Chapter 17: The Future of the Digital Age

As Olanna and Kelechi looked towards the future, they remained hopeful and optimistic about the possibilities of the digital age. They understood that the rapid advancements in technology would continue to shape the world, presenting both opportunities and challenges.

They remained committed to their values, seeking to use technology for the greater good. Olanna continued to advocate for ethical practices in the tech industry, promoting innovation that prioritized human well-being and sustainability. She believed that technology could be a force for positive change if guided by compassion and integrity.

Kelechi also pursued his dreams, leveraging technology to create solutions that addressed pressing global issues. Together, they envisioned a future where technology and humanity coexisted harmoniously, creating a world that was more connected, inclusive, and equitable.

Their journey was a testament to the power of balance in the digital age. Olanna and Kelechi had navigated the complexities of their careers, love, and faith with grace and resilience. Their legacy was one of compassion, integrity, and unwavering commitment to making a positive impact on the world. As they embraced the future, they remained hopeful and inspired, ready to face whatever challenges and opportunities lay ahead.

Artificial Dreams, Eternal Callings: Balancing Career, Love, and Faith in the Digital Age

In **"Artificial Dreams, Eternal Callings,"** Olanna's journey through the digital age is a captivating exploration of ambition, love, and spirituality. Set against the backdrop of Lagos's bustling tech hub, Olanna thrives as a pioneering tech professional, pushing the boundaries of innovation. However, her relentless pursuit of career success leaves her questioning the true essence of fulfillment.

Enter Kelechi, a fellow tech enthusiast, whose intellectual prowess and heartfelt support help Olanna navigate the intricate dance between professional ambitions and personal life. Their love story unfolds amidst virtual meetings and distant travels, highlighting the challenges and rewards of maintaining a relationship in an era dominated by technology.

Faith emerges as Olanna's guiding light, offering solace and clarity in a world overwhelmed by digital noise. Through church services, community involvement, and shared spiritual growth with Kelechi, she discovers that faith, love, and career need not be mutually exclusive. Instead, they can coexist harmoniously, offering her a sense of purpose and balance.

As Olanna mentors the next generation of tech professionals, her legacy of resilience, compassion, and integrity begins to take shape. Her story is a testament to the power of balance and the importance of staying true to one's values, even in the face of the relentless pace of the digital age.

"Artificial Dreams, Eternal Callings" is an inspiring tale of self-discovery, highlighting the delicate equilibrium between career aspirations, enduring love, and unwavering faith. It serves as a reminder that in the age of technology, the human spirit remains resilient, seeking connection, meaning, and harmony.

www.ingramcontent.com/pod-product-compliance
Lightning Source LLC
LaVergne TN
LVHW020742090526
838202LV00057BA/6196